M is for MOHAWK

An Alphabet Book of Fresh Hairstyles
by Dr. Tamara Pizzoli

For Noah and Milo

and for Marcus Sobczak,
who came up with something for the
letter I

Copyright © 2015 by Tamara Pizzoli
www.theenglishschoolhouse.com

ISBN: 978-0-9960016-6-3

Cover Design and Illustration by Howell Edwards Creative

M is for MOHAWK

An Alphabet Book of Fresh Hairstyles
by Dr. Tamara Pizzoli

A is for AFRO

B is for BEEHIVE

C is for COMBOVER

D is for DREADS

E is for EDGE-UP

F is for FINGER WAVES

G is for GOATEE

H is for HIGHTOP

I is for INDUCTION CUT

J is for JHERI CURL

K is for KINKY TWISTS

L is for LIBERTY SPIKES

M is for MOHAWK

N is for NUBIAN LOCS

O is for OSELEDETS

P is for POMPADOUR

Q is for QUEUE

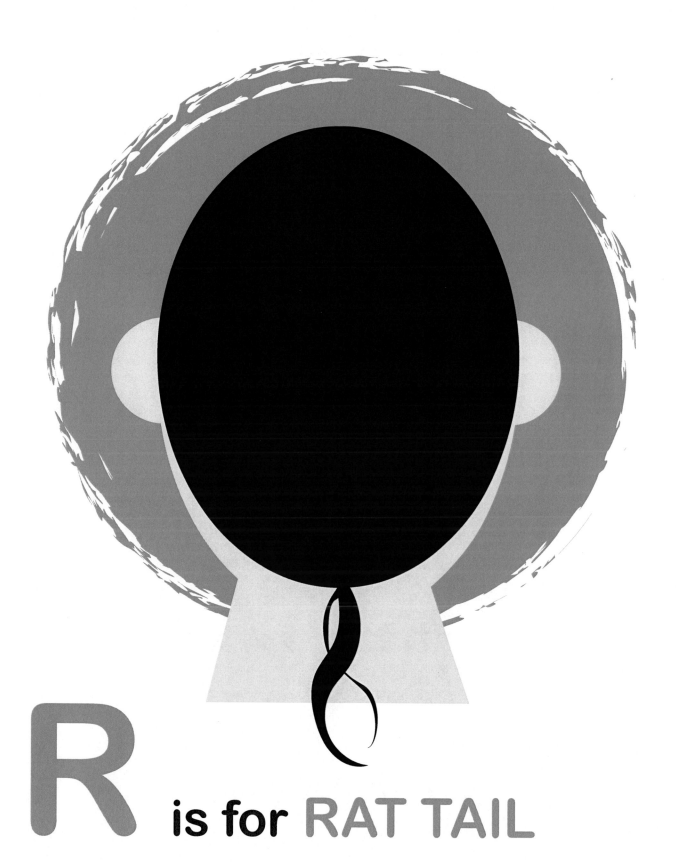

R is for RAT TAIL

S is for SHAG

T is for Tonsure

U is for UP-DO

V is for V layer cut

W is for WAVES

X is for EXTRA LONG

Y is for YOUR HAIR (Draw it!)

Z is for ZEE END (and the end)

M is for Mohawk:
An Alphabet Book of Fresh Hairstyles

is a fun and funky tour through the abc's of hairdos.

Enjoy the simultaneously diverse and uniform illustrations on each page.

And get in on the fun by drawing your own hairstyle for letter Y.

Made in the USA
Middletown, DE
31 January 2016